## *Act Like a CEO, Think Like a Millionaire:*
Why You Should Care *LESS* about What a Man or Woman Thinks About Love, Intimacy, and Commitment and *MORE* about *GETTING WHAT YOU WANT OUT OF LIFE*

## Also by **T.R. Ipleac**

*What You Won't Expect When You're Expecting Because This is The CRAP They Don't Tell You: ABC's of a SUCKY Pregnancy*

## *Act Like a CEO, Think Like a Millionaire:*

Why You Should Care *LESS* about What a Man or Woman Thinks About Love, Intimacy, and Commitment and *MORE* about *GETTING WHAT YOU WANT OUT OF LIFE*

By T.R. Ipleac

Copyright © 2012 T.R. Ipleac

All rights reserved. Published in the United States and Internationally by TTP Publishing.

No part of this book may be reproduced or transmitted in any form or by any means without written permission from the author.

ISBN: 978-0-9904430-2-5.

## *Act Like a CEO, Think Like a Millionaire:*
Why You Should Care LESS about What a Man or Woman Thinks About Love, Intimacy, and Commitment and MORE about *GETTING WHAT YOU WANT OUT OF LIFE*

By T.R. Ipleac

This book is dedicated to women everywhere.

There is no need for mind games.

It's simple: DO YOU. GET HIM.

# Introduction

I love Steve Harvey. That man is all kinds of funny. I listen to his morning show and literally laugh out loud. I laugh so hard in the mornings that my four year old laughs too, and says, "Mommy, you're silly!" I mean, I love me some Steve Harvey. And I support him. However, as much as I love him, I think he is a bit off in his focus with his book, *Act Like a Woman, Think Like a Man*. Here is the thing, and I'm just keeping it real: Women, if you have to ask, wonder, and question what a man wants and/or how to get one, then you are already up a creek and without a paddle. In other words, you're in trouble.

Real women, *confident women*, don't wonder about these things, at least not to the point of needing to read about it or study it. The reason real women don't need this information is because we are too busy running our businesses and making our money. And funny enough, we have never (or rarely) been without a man. Here's the reason why: A man can smell desperation[1]. He can feel it. Desperation is like bacon. Everybody, regardless of their station in life or where they reside in the world, can recognize the smell of bacon. The same holds true for desperation.

I am not saying that wanting a man is desperate. Quite the contrary, wanting the companionship of a man is not only normal, it is necessary. After all, we are social beings and we were not created to be alone. But needing to follow some rules or guidelines to "snatch up one of these hot commodities" is silly and sad. If you are about your business, doing your thing, and getting all that you want and deserve out of life, nine times out of ten you

---

[1] One of my husband's ex-girlfriends is one of those women who still calls his momma and tries to "stay in the family". But I can't blame her, because my husband is a beautiful, hard-working, wife-pleasing, child-raising, putting-it-down type of man. Still, desperation smells, ladies. So if you are guilty of desperately trying to hold on to someone by staying in their circle, or family, move on. You cannot move forward if you are looking behind you. Furthermore, while you are looking behind you, you might miss the man who is in front of you - the one that's actually meant for you.

will have and/or get everything you need, and that includes a good man. If you have to audition for one, or study them as you would a final exam in college, then you have work to do - ON YOURSELF.

The effort you are taking to read about how a man loves, thinks, forms relationships, etcetera, could be spent on reading a book on turning your great idea into a business, turning your small business into a bigger one, and most of all, turning yourself into a CEO. The men, the money, the luxurious life, the vacations, the self-confident children, the legacy – all of this will come. And the rest is for the birds. Because why should you care that your man needs to find himself before he looks for you? Why aren't you also finding yourself before you look for him? Or better yet, before you let him find you?

I love Steve's description of the building of a man. But let me reverse that and discuss the building of a woman. From the time we are girls, heck, from the time we are infants, we are put in pink bows, and given frilly dresses and pretty curls and told to be small, be quiet, be still, be pretty, don't be too loud, be soft, don't be rough, be muted. How many of us have heard, "Girls don't talk that loud!" "Put some shoes on before you get big feet! No man is going to want a woman with big feet!"

We are told not to fight. We are told not to get dirty. We are told not to be too bold. We are given baby dolls to aid in our training to be sensitive, in preparation for our roles as caregivers. We know how to garden, paint our nails and toenails, and style our hair before we reach puberty. As little girls, we get grocery shopping carts, dresses for our dolls, and tea sets as gifts. This reinforces for us the expectation that we should cook for our family, keep our children clean, and be delicate. After all, girls are made of sugar and spice and all things nice.

This expectation continues as we get older, when we are made to care for our younger siblings, to help mom around the house. From the time we receive our first baby doll, our lives as caregivers and moms are cemented, to the point that if we choose not to have children people assume that something is wrong with us, or that we couldn't find a man to procreate with. Those of us who only have sons, or God forbid have no children at all are asked, "Why, who's going to take care of you when you get old?" We are asked this ridiculous question with a straight face.

Well, I say Bull-you-know-what! Apparently, we will not get a good man until he has figured out who he is, what he is, and how much money he should or wants to make. Ok, but what about us? Once he figures that out, should we then line ourselves up in our pretty pink dresses and wait to be chosen? Should we wait until he has found himself so that we can be found also? And once we're found, then what? Is it our privilege to give him children and a clean house? Is it our privilege to obediently sit beside him as he claims us like one would a stray dog from the pound? Are we to get excited that once he's claimed us and professed his love (as Steve says he should), that he now wants to pay our bills? I'd much prefer we have the resources to pay our own bills - outright. No monthly payment plan, no credit cards. Just pure cash money. Because that's how successful people do it. And if we concern ourselves with ensuring our success, and becoming everything we want to be, then we'll get the rest. And that includes the man.

Let me be clear. This book is not to insult women, or to suggest we don't need men. We need them, and we like them, and no one is meant to be alone. Far from insulting women, this book is meant to insist that we are more than we think, more than we give ourselves credit for. Also, that if we put half as much energy into realizing who we are, what it is we're capable of, and our own potential, then we can become wealthy, successful, great women. It is then that we will meet the man/men of our dreams. Not a day or a paycheck before.

## Birds of a Feather Flock Together

We've all heard this proverb before, but let's see how it applies to our success and acquisition of personal fulfillment and getting a man. How many medical doctors do you know that are married to strippers? How many front desk hotel clerks do you know who are married to research scientists? Now, I am not insulting any professions. To each his own, as I was once a front desk hotel clerk while in college before going on to graduate school and obtaining my Ph.D. and becoming a successful entrepreneur, among other things. And although I've never been a stripper, my husband can attest to the fact that I have an inner stripper. I think all of us women do. By the way, yes, my inner stripper has a name, and no, I won't tell you what it is. That story is for another day.

Eliminating the exceptions to the rule - because there will always be someone who will fit the unusual profile, and I do not want any letters from ex-strippers telling me about their cardiologist husband - my point is that we are often like the people who are in our company. If we hang around bums, we are probably going to be a bum. That is, if we're not already. Likewise, if we hang around successful people, we are probably ourselves successful, or at least on our way there.

The same goes for developing personal relationships and finding a man. If we become successful entrepreneurs, we are likely to go to places where other successful entrepreneurs are: conferences, seminars, etcetera. This increases our chances of meeting and marrying a fellow successful entrepreneur. Not because we are looking, but because this is who is in our social circle.

Studies show that an increasing number of black women are marrying men outside of their race or entering into interracial relationships. I don't think this is because these women are looking for men outside of their race. I think it is because black women are going further and further academically, and are thus encountering more and more men outside of their race. Don't kill the messenger, but the sad fact is that, statistically, black men do not go as far academically as black women. I think this has a lot to do with the social and political climate of our country, but that story is for another day. The point is, because educated black women are sometimes more so in the company of white men, they are thus socializing with these men and developing relationships with them.

Think about it, if you are in graduate school, you are likely to meet and marry someone in graduate school, or at least with a college education, because that is where you hang out and it's the type of person you encounter. Similarly, what do you think happens if you work a job where you barely make ends meet? Or are in a situation where you are doing nothing with your life? Nine times out of ten, you are going to meet a similar type of person because you'll be in each other's circles. That broke guy who doesn't work is not going to hang out at medical conferences, because that's not his thing. And although that medical doctor might frequent the strip club, he is not going to marry that girl. He might freak her. But he's likely going to go home to a wife that he considers to have a higher caliber.

What's the point of this information? Get a higher caliber of existence and meet people who are on that same level. Remain low-level and don't be surprised when you meet low-level people. Now, of course you can hang around places where "good men" might be. But what are you all going to talk about? When he wants to discuss art and culture, and politics, what are you going to do? You can sex a man real good all you want, but eventually, when you all get out of the bed, he's going to know if you're stupid. And nobody wants a stupid woman (or man), because stupid ain't cute. A real man, a good man worth his salt, won't want a stupid woman. Especially when he can get a successful woman who will still put it on him, AND can get out of bed and have a great conversation. Men like successful women. Don't think for a second that they do not.

Take my husband and I as examples. We are both research scientists with Ph.Ds. When people meet us, they are often impressed that both he and I have doctorates. But it's really not that big of a deal. The simple fact is that we were both in graduate school at the same place, at around the same time, and we met there. And let me share this with you. My husband - a gorgeous, intelligent, athletically-built, ridiculously sexy man - is a few years older than I. He got to graduate school a few years ahead of me. While there, he had a girlfriend. She was not in graduate school; she was in college but later flunked out. When I came on the scene, bustin' balls and confident, with guys falling at my feet, he dropped her like a bad habit for a *chance* to get with me.

Now, of course I didn't know he'd had a girl that he dropped when the opportunity to get with me presented itself. I found this out after the fact. But he's since then told me that he couldn't help himself; that from the first day he saw me, then got to know me, he had to try to make me his. He has told me that even though he saw how I was shutting other guys down, that he had to give getting with me a try. Now, many happy years and a couple kids later, the rest is history. But my point is, confidence matters, being about your business matters, not appearing concerned about catching a good man is noticed by good men. See, I wasn't concerned about meeting a man. I was concerned about becoming a doctor, about making my mark in the world, and as such, I couldn't shake the guys who were interested. Where will you be and what will you be doing when you meet your Mr. Right? Hopefully you'll be about your business so you can meet a man that's about his.

**What are your dreams?**

No disrespect to Steve, or anyone else out there, but if as a woman or a young woman your version of "The dream" is "The husband, some kids, a house" then you have big problems[2].

Whatever happened to your own identity? I am a factual woman, and I appreciate honesty, so you will always get it straight from me. What I am about to report might shock some, while others will nod

---

[2] I am not speaking of those women whose only dream is, in fact, to have a husband and children. To each her own. I am not judging you, nor declaring that you aren't living your full potential. Indeed, I cannot decide what your full potential is. In fact, I am probably a combination of you (the stay-at-home mom) and the mighty working woman, in that I seek a key role in the raising of my children and personal care of my family, AND I also want to conquer the world professionally. As I said, to each her own. My only problem would be if you want to do more, and feel you should be something more, and you drop your dreams because you let society tell you that a husband and children are what makes a woman. If you subscribe to that mentality because you don't have the balls, or *ovaries* to think otherwise, then we need to talk. If this is you, and you want my help to reach what you feel is your full potential, I am a click away. Email me at **info@ttppublishing.com**. We'll see if we can't figure it out together.

their head in agreement, as if to say, "Well, duh!" A recent study showed that some women, many women in fact, did not like spending time with their own children. One of the things they reported preferring to do is grocery shop! Now, this is not my position. Indeed, I put my intended career on hold to personally raise my children, but I most certainly understand where these women are coming from. I think the women in the study (and some women in general) aren't enjoying spending time with their children as much because at times it feels like a job. It is certainly not an identity. No job is an identity.

As an Obstetrician, what you do is deliver babies. It is not who you are. As a lawyer or an attorney, what you do is practice law. It is not who you are. Having children is what you did. So, who are you? If, in your opinion, a mom is all you are, then what were you before they came around? Were you invalid? Being a mom might be your most significant role - I know it is for me - but it is not who you are. And a wife? It sucks for you if your identity is wrapped up in being a wife because, according to the

2009 U.S. Census, there is a nearly 20% chance that your marriage will end in a divorce or separation of some sort. As well as an almost 30% chance that you'll never get married in the first place. So if you don't have wife as an identity, what will you have then?

To some women, the title "wife" means the world. You know the women I'm talking about. You often hear them say, "That's my huzzzzzband". "My huzzzzzband thinks this, my huzzzzzband says that." They mention their husbands more than they do themselves. His accomplishments, what he said, what he thinks. Instead of envying this woman, I think I would feel pity because she's so busy being his wife that she fails to be herself.

And if you are this woman, think about why that man fell in love with you. Were you smart? Feisty? In your own place handling your business? What makes you think he no longer wants that? Sure, he might like that you have softened and now depend, to an extent, on him in your life. But no man wants a weak, inconsequential woman. No man wants to sit up and talk all night because you have no friends, you only have him. He is your world. No man wants to watch romantic movies all night long, or hear your thoughts on your feelings all day. That's what your girlfriends are for. But if you don't have any friends, or a social life, or an identity of your own, then that man has to become your everything. He's got to be your girlfriend, your stylist, your personal assistant, your therapist. Girl, get a life…YOUR OWN!

    I firmly believe that the only time a happy life and true love will come is when you love yourself enough to want to make it happy for yourself. True love will come, from others, when you love your own company first. After all, if you can't stand to be alone in your own company, then what man will want to? Let me reiterate - because sometimes as women we hear what we want to hear - I'm not against true love, but I don't think it can be true and fulfilling if you aren't fulfilled. And I think unless it's what you exclusively set out for in life, having a husband and some kids will not fulfill your personal goals. Get it for yourself, girl.

Ladies - and men who also want to realize their full potential and get what they want out of life - if you need a playbook, here it is. The rules are simple:

1. Games are for children, and mind games are for teenagers and jeopardy contestants. Successful adults, CEOs, keep it real. What CEO do you know that beats around the bush? They get to the point. They do what needs to be done. And they handle their business.
2. If you are looking for love, try looking to do *what* you love and loving to do what brings you personal success and financial prosperity.

Just to be clear, financial prosperity doesn't have to mean making millions. It's sad that I have to put that qualifier in here, but if I do not somebody somewhere will get upset because I dared to tell them they could or should make millions. It amazes me that some people get offended by the idea of being successful. Financial prosperity means being able to comfortably care for your family. In my opinion, PAYING A BILL FOR 30 YEARS (mortgage) is not comfortably caring for your family. In my opinion, PAYING A BILL FOR 20 YEARS (school loans) is not comfortably caring for your family. It is equivalent to be an indentured servant. The deal we strike with the government, in my mind, goes something like this, "You (Sallie Mae) pay for my education and I (indentured servant) will work for the rest of my life - probably in a job I don't even like - to pay you back. If not the rest of my life, then I'll at least work for you for nearly a quarter of a century." Thanks, but no thanks.

That money could be going elsewhere, if you had been able to PAY OFF your house. Or if you had been able to privately fund your own education. That is what I mean by financial prosperity. That is what I want for my sons, for myself and my husband, and for you. You should also want it for yourself. If you don't, then don't be mad at me for wanting it.

There are people out there who make $20,000^3$, or even less, a year. If you are looking for love, then maybe that's a good thing, because it's going to take at least two people to make any type of living if one or more of them is only making a few hundred dollars a week.

I don't mean to be cold. I mean to be honest, and real. Maybe instead of looking for a man, you should be looking for an opportunity to flaunt what you got. I'm talking about your skills. We all have a hidden CEO inside of us. And we all have something in us that can make us rich. There are people who have made a hairstyle using a bobby pin, and are now

---

[3] Please save the emails, as somebody somewhere is going to email me and tell me that they raised 59 children on $58. 29. They are then going to insist that money is not necessary to live a full life. To them I will say, "That's great! I am happy for you that you were able to do so much for so little. But for the rest of us, those whose marriages failed because of money problems, or those whose families go hungry because their low-level jobs don't pay them enough to live on, but pays them too much to seek assistance, we want more and better for our children than what we had for ourselves. So kindly step out of our way as we pursue our destinies. Thanks!"

millionaires. How many times did you flip your hair, and get your "do" right, simply using a bobby pin? That million dollar idea could have been yours.

Others have made millions baking cookies, designing hair care products, teaching others how to hold in their guts? How many times have people told you your baking is good enough to make them want to slap their mommas? How many creams have you concocted in the kitchen that has calmed even the most unruly kitchens (for the novices out there, "kitchen" refers to the stubborn or fly-away hair at the nape of a woman's neck), and how young were you when you started using that special material/shirt/or fabric as a great hold-it-all-in undergarment? That million dollar idea could have been yours. That millionaire could've been you. It should've been you! It could STILL become you. You just have to refocus your energy.

Put your time and attention into becoming the best you. And if you do that then you will succeed. A great side benefit might also be finding a wonderful person to share your life with. And by the way, it's not that becoming successful will ensure that you find a significant other. But think about this, if you had to be lonely wouldn't you much rather be lonely and wealthy/self-actualized than lonely and broke? I'm just saying.

Furthermore, like I always tell the young and not-so-young people I provide services to: you only get one life. Why waste it? You do NOT get to make nickels and dimes and struggle during this lifetime and think, "Oh well, next time I'll do it right and make something of myself." Nope. You only get one shot. And I'm willing to bet that, as a child, you probably didn't think, "Well, I can't wait to grow up and get a barely-there job, or a career that cost more to obtain (loans) than it pays in wages."

No one plans to grow up and take thirty years to own a home – that is, if they can even afford to get to that point - or to live check-to-check. We all dream of financial prosperity. We dream of living comfortably, of providing for our families. (Yes,

Steve, believe it or not, women also want to provide for their families). For most of us, our dreams don't stop at a husband and some kids. Question is, when did you stop dreaming?

But some of us are already successful. So, even if success is not what you want, if you are satisfied with where you are in life, even if all you seek is a solid relationship but just can't figure out how to get one; or if you want a better relationship, I would STILL challenge you to start with yourself. If you seek a solid relationship, develop one with yourself first. Take yourself out to dinner. Go see a movie. Take up dancing, even without a partner.

Keep up with yourself. Get a mani-pedi even if no one will see it. Get a bikini wax (ouch!) or wear pretty lingerie to bed even if no one will get to enjoy it but you. When you take care of yourself, cherish yourself, you tell others this is what you expect. Steve was right about standards. They are necessary. They are the lesson plans that teach others how to treat us, based on how we expect to be treated. But Steve says you can't take it from me because I am a woman. Well, here are my stats. I am a successful, highly educated woman who is happily married, with a Ph.D., a thriving consulting business, a couple books in the works, organizations that help youth (non-profit) and adults (for-profit) start their own businesses, a husband who also holds a Ph.D. and a six-figure income, with 2 beautiful children. And I just turned thirty only three days ago. This means that I had achieved all these things that I consider to be great successes while I was still in my 20's.

Now that I am 30, there is even more life to live, goals to accomplish, and success to be had. So if you are looking for a good man, with a JOB, who actually takes care of and provides for his kids, who knocks your socks off sexually, leads you spiritually, and challenges you mentally, all while spoiling the hell out of you, then take it from me. If you aren't looking for that kind of man, and aren't looking to go any further in life, then kindly return this book to its file, or shelf. No offense taken. Good luck and God bless.

For the rest of us….Despite the long introduction, these chapters will be succinct and to the point, because whether we are looking for a man or looking for a million, we all have things to do. Time is money. And I don't know that we can ever have enough of either. So, let's get started.

## Chapter 1: *LOVE*... What You Do and Do What You Love

**What is your hobby?**

Introduction

People spend an average of one-third of their lives working. Yet only 45% report enjoying what they do. Many have done what they are doing for so long, that they no longer realize what they even enjoy doing anymore. So, let's take this first crucial step together.

**Activity 1: Grab a piece of paper and ask, then answer, these questions:** *If money wasn't an issue, what would you do if you could do anything at all?*

For me that answer has always been to help others. When I was a child I thought I could do this by becoming a Pediatrician. I was young so I thought I'd start with young people. At the age of eight, after a fundraising activity in which I generated enough money to feed some homeless people that lived under the bridge near a popular intersection in my hometown (I bought hamburgers from McDonald's on Wednesdays when they were 29 cents) it confirmed my love for helping others, but it also showed me that I did not want to provide medical help. I wanted to provide social help. Additionally, it showed me that I wanted to help young and older people.

As I grew older, I saw a lot of young girls become pregnant as teenagers. This bothered me, and I began to wonder, "Why them and not me?" Especially since we had all come from the same neighborhoods? I decided to become a Psychologist, so that I could explore what caused a young girl to decide to become a teenage mom and/or drop out of school. As a result, young women were added to the list of people I wanted to help. In high school and college I volunteered and worked with organizations that provided services to young women. I also developed and implemented a teenage pregnancy and STD prevention program that was picked up by some local and national nonprofit organizations. I graduated with a Bachelor's Degree, with Honors, in Psychology and went on to pursue a Ph.D. in Counseling Psychology.

While in graduate school I developed and implemented intervention and educational programs, and provided counseling to a broad range of clients. The program development I loved, the one-on-one counseling I didn't love so much, which showed me that counseling was not what I wanted to do. Although I still wanted to help others - particularly the disadvantaged, young women, and youth - I wanted to help them on a broader scale and not just individually with one-on-one counseling sessions. On the other hand, I lived for developing and designing programs and curriculum that enhanced the lives of others.

So, after 2 years and 69 hours of doctoral work in Psychology, I retested and reapplied to a different Ph.D. program in Public Administration and Public Policy. This program would allow me to help many others by designing intervention and educational programs that enhanced their lives and allowed them to better their circumstances. And all these years later, this is STILL the work I do and the work that I love. I design, develop, and often implement programs and curriculum that enhance the lives of others.

Having gone to school as long as I have, and realizing the potential of entrepreneurship OVER education, these programs are often entrepreneurial in nature. But many still deal with social ailments, such as teenage pregnancy and STD prevention, as well as educational and racial disparities, but it all began from doing what I loved.

So spend some time exploring what you simply love to do - whether or not it comes with a paycheck. Because in a later section of the book, I will help you figure out how to get paid to do what you love.

For this activity, ask yourself, "What do I love to do so much that I would do it for free?" A great way to do this exercise, and explore this question, is to sit somewhere very quietly with your eyes closed and ask yourself what you were doing the last time you truly enjoyed yourself. Were you picking flowers, were you sewing, were you reading a book?

This activity will provide a hint, and some insight, into what your interest/passion might be. For example, were you reading last? Maybe you'd like to write a book, as reading and writing usually go hand-in-hand. Were you picking a flower? Maybe you'd like to own a flower shop. Were you sewing something? Maybe you'd like to own a seamstress shop, or be a clothing designer/manufacturer.

## What Do You Do Well?

## What Do *Others* Tell You That You Do Well?

Part 2: What are you good at?

Now it's time to figure out what you're good at. Here's how to do that. What do others come to you for, or ask your help with? DO NOT GET THIS CONFUSED WITH WHAT YOU'D DO IF YOU COULD DO ANYTHING (your passion). Your skills are what you do well, even if it annoys you to do it. And don't be surprised if it does in fact annoy you – it might annoy you simply because others come to you so frequently for it. For example, do others come to you to get their hair done? Do they ask for your advice when picking out something to wear for a special event? Do others come to you for advice? What kind of advice?

For example, one of my good friends often has people come to her for marital advice, even though her Master's Degree is in School Psychometry. She has helped restore and/or put together many happy marriages. The fact that others come to her for this, and she does it with success, is an example of finding what you're good at.

Have you ever heard of, or read, the bible verses that translate into "You can tell a tree by the fruit it bears" (Matthew 7:16-20; 12:33; Luke 6:43-45)? How this scripture applies to finding what you're good at, is that when you are good at something there will be proof. If you are a good hairstylist, you will have a great many clients. If you are a good preacher, you will probably have a packed church. If people come to you for something, and RETURN, then that probably means you did what you do successfully. The proof is in the pudding, or in this case, in the fruit.

Keep in mind that what you're good at, and often called on for, can be different from what is your hobby or what you like to do. Be aware of this. But do not run from it. It is often a clue, and can be an indication of the steps you should follow to get where you want to be. Case in point, I love to read. There is nothing more relaxing and enjoyable than a good book and an overcast day, or a good book and some ice cream, or a good book and a fireplace. The common denominator is the good book.

What others come to me for, however, is help. They want advice on fixing problems. They seek counsel on helping their teenager stay out of trouble, helping themselves become entrepreneurs, or helping their organization to become more effective. I thought I was paying attention to the clues, but really I was misreading them. Initially, I only looked at my capacity to help others in an individualized way. People came to me with a wide range of problems, so I thought I'd become a Psychologist. Halfway through the Psychology Ph.D. program, I realized that it was not a good fit. In part, it was not a good fit because I am a problem solver, a "get-in-there-and-make-it-happen or make-it-work kind of person. Therapy does not work like that.

In Psychology, a Therapist/Psychologist/Counselor does not solve problems per se; they help others reach insight into their problems, by making connections between their thoughts and actions, or between past trauma and current behavior or psychoses. Also, I wanted to help lots of people, and not one every hour like is typically done in a therapy/counseling session. A talk with a trusted advisor and a change of doctoral programs landed me right where I needed to be.

With a doctorate, and thus expertise, in Public Administration and Public Policy, I am able to design intervention programs that help whole groups of people or communities solve issues. I am able to go into organizations and perform assessments that identify their weaknesses and strengths and develop programs that help them (1) address those weaknesses and (2) promote those strengths. I am able to work with people one at a time, in groups, in organizations, and even nationally to help them reach their potential through entrepreneurship. In a nutshell, I am able to do me. Yet, I was still missing a component.

After I had one of my children, and because I don't believe in paying another to raise them, I decided to stay at home and work from home. Well, my ability to reach others, personally, was compromised, as it became too difficult to set up consultations with a newborn in tow, especially one as fat and cuddly as my little guy. So I began to write down what all I would do when he was older and I was back in the workforce. I also began to turn back to some of the fictional pieces I had started to write on and off again throughout my college and graduate years. And I realized a few things: (1) I still truly loved to read and write (obviously, since I spent so many years in school), (2) I was good at it, and (3) I could use it to help others, either in developing programs that would still allow me to reach my clients, but I could also use my writing to tell stories and entertain the masses.

Once I realized that I could incorporate all of me into my dreams and goals, that indeed I should, the opportunities became limitless. I even have an Entrepreneurial Institute in the works that will teach others everything they need from start to finish to start a business. Mostly all from home.

For more information, send me an email to **info@ttppublishing.com** (put HELP in the Subject line), and I will send you information on how to access the Institute's services.

The point is that I had finally learned to merge my love of writing and reading with what I am good at, which is helping others. Although I got detoured along the way, as you may also, I was able to use every experience to get me where I wanted to be, which is exactly where I am. Though I'm not stopping here. And neither should you!

## How to Monetize it?

Now that you've rediscovered what you like to do, and merged it with what you do well - as confirmed by others - the next step is to make it profitable.

Using myself as an example, I, of course, sell my books. I charge consultation fees to my clients, and am in the process of designing a full-on curriculum that will allow me to reach a larger audience. The point is to bring your services to others. If you bake, sell your goodies. You can do it online. You can try to develop relationships and ultimately contacts with local or even national bakeries and grocery stores to see if they might want to distribute your product. In this age of personal advertisement through social media, there is really no limit to how you can market yourself and your products. You just have to start.

If you tutor, advertise yourself locally as a tutor. Or send me your information and what your subject matter is, and I might hire you to develop a program for the Entrepreneurial Institute. If you cut or do hair, make some business cards and hand them out at the mall, thus advertising your services. Go to places where people might be. Grocery stores, the movies, the park. And definitely go to the places where people want to look their best: church, wedding stores to find future brides, malls, etcetera.

You get my point. If you sew, do the same thing. Go to the malls and hand out cards to teenage girls. One of them might want a prom dress made. If you do makeup, nails, follow the same steps. If you have a specialized skill, advertise yourself as a consultant. If you are still unsure how to make what you do, or want to do, work for you, then shoot me an email to **info@ttppublishing.com** and I'll see if I can help you out. The point is (1) to find what you like, (2) confirm through others that you do it well (if more people followed this step then American Idol would lose a ton of performers, but we would also lose the fun that goes along with watching those initial hopefuls), (3) begin to do it (which helps iron out the kinks) (4) and market/advertise to others that you do it. Then, as you're making your money, watch Suzie Orman to figure out how to spend it wisely, save it carefully, and grow it abundantly.

## LLC, YOU: Step Out on Faith and Go For it!

Once you're running whatever service you've decided to provide, for at least a little while, and have ironed out the kinks, legitimize it. Learn the difference between an Inc., LLC, S-Corporation, C-Corporation, a Partnership, or a Sole Proprietorship. Do not be detoured. Do not be shaken. You will be scared, but do not let it stop you. You will make mistakes, learn from them. The point is, you miss 100% of the shots you don't take. So take a shot.

After all, what can you lose other than the ability to call yourself broke? To blame the economy for your present circumstance? The use of excuses to explain why you aren't all that you thought you'd be? The guilt you feel at raising your child in a neighborhood you don't trust or in a school that does more harm than good? I am obviously being facetious, but the point is, you can only make yourself better. So try your hand at bettering your life.

## Chapter 2: Develop RELATIONSHIPS With, or Study, the People Who Can Help You Get to Where You Want to Be

### Crabs in a Barrel

I am willing to bet that we have all experienced crabs at least once in our lives. Get your minds out of the gutter, people. I am talking about those crabs that want you to stay down with them. They are the kinds of people who try to pull you back down with them when you try to rise above your station in life. If you haven't experienced a crab, then you are lucky. Or maybe you just haven't done anything worth anyone trying to pull you down for. But if you are ready to start doing your thing and getting your life together, then get ready to meet some crabs.

Below is a presentation of different types of crabs. As you read about these different types of crabs, keep in mind that this book is meant to help get you motivated to accomplish whatever it is you want, whether that's finding a mate, starting a business, going back to school, or getting out of debt. With those scenarios in mind, let's meet the crabs.

**Girlfriend Crab**

The girlfriend crab is used to you being single with her. She's used to the two of you going out together, or at a minimum, she's used to the two of you male-bashing together. A common theme throughout your relationship with this crab might be, "Girl, all men suck!"

So, lo and behold, you meet a man. And for the sake of argument, let's say that he is a good man. But as is the case in real life, let's say that he lacks one of the things you thought you wanted in a man. Let's say that he is 5 foot 10 instead of the six-foot guy you thought you wanted, or that he works at the library instead of being the lawyer you thought you'd bring home. Girlfriend Crab will be the person to say, "Girl, he's not tall enough for you!" Or, "Girl, he doesn't make enough money!"

Maybe Girlfriend Crab doesn't mean to be spiteful, or maybe she does. It doesn't really matter. The point is that she doesn't want you to leave her behind. She doesn't want you to leave the station of life that you're in. So her goal is to keep you single as long as she single. That's Girlfriend Crab.

**Colleague Crab**

You and Colleague Crab have shared a cubicle for a number of years. You two might make lunch runs together. You two might help each other complete assignments. And you two, most assuredly, complain about the boss together.

One day you decide that you no longer want a boss. You decide that you want to go into business for yourself. Somebody told you that you had the best pound cakes ever made, and you decide you want to turn baking pound cakes into a business. Colleague Crab will tell you that you're crazy. Colleague Crab will tell you that you don't have enough money to start a business. Colleague Crab will tell you that you don't have enough experience to start a business.

Colleague Crab will tell you that you are dreaming and to get real. S/he will point out that you never even finished high school, and as such, you certainly don't have the first idea how to run a business. The truth is, Colleague Crab is scared. Colleague Crab realizes that if you start a business you could possibly achieve success. And Colleague Crab doesn't want to be left behind. Moreover, Colleague Crab does not want to look up in five years and still be in the same position she's in while you are now a CEO. That's Colleague Crab.

**Warden Crab**

If you decide that you want to go back to school, Warden Crab reminds you that school is expensive, that you have kids now and thus different priorities, that you never were good at school, and that you will have to spend your weekends doing homework. Warden Crab does everything s/he can to keep you out of school and away from possibly bettering yourself. Especially since he or she has always wanted to go back to school themselves. They certainly don't want you to beat them to the punch.

## Bougie Crab

When you tell Bougie Crab that you're going to start saving your money because your goal is to get out of debt, Bougie Crab thinks you're crazy for shopping at Walmart. Bougie Crab gets upset when you don't want to join her for lunch, because you've chosen instead to bring your lunch from home. Bougie Crab sneers when your children are not wearing the latest Jordans.

Bougie Crab frowns when you don't go get your hair done every week. S/he has something to say about the car you drive, the house you live in, and what you do with your money. The truth is, Bougie Crab is probably credit-maxed out of her behind, but she doesn't want you to know. What she wants instead is for you to join her in Debtland. She wants the two of you to be full of debt and full of Prada. She wants both of you to have Nada.

And there are many more types of crabs. There's a Weight-Loss Crab that as soon as you decide you want to get in shape, s/he starts to bring you all types of sweets and desserts. There's the Divorce Crab that tries to dissuade you from working on your marriage. She reminds you that your husband did you wrong a while ago and that there is plenty more fish in the sea. Truth is, she probably wishes she also had a chance to fix her own home. But her husband probably doesn't want her - or the marriage - anymore. Or at a minimum, she wishes you two were both raising your children in single-parent households.

Moreover, there are even the crabs that want to dissuade you from going to church. In sum, there are way too many crabs to name. The point is to get rid of the crabs. You don't have to bring them with you, you don't have to convince them that what you're doing is right, and you don't even have to tell them what your plan is. Crabs are destructive, they are intimidating, and they draw on our insecurities and take advantage of our weaknesses. They are no good, and if left unchecked, will wreak havoc in our lives.

Get rid of them. And if you can't get rid of them (as in the case of in-laws, for example), then minimize their importance in your life, minimize their influence on your decisions, and eliminate their ability to hold you from your destiny. After all, nobody wants crabs. If someone is not for you that means they're against you. No ifs, ands, buts….. or crabs.

## Stalk…by Television and Social Media

You ever hear the saying, "You are what you eat?" Well, I believe the same holds true for what you watch and what you hear. If you listen to meditational CDs all day, then you're probably going to be extremely relaxed and clear-headed. If you listen to rap music all day, then you're probably going to feel all riled up. Why is it that we listen to upbeat music before we go out to the club? It's to get us in the mood for dancing and being upbeat. Why is it that we listen to gospel when we're down? It's to lift our spirits and remind us of the goodness of God. Why is it that we listen to soft music as we prepare to get intimate with our partner? It's to get us in the mood.

The same holds true for what we watch. You ever see an elementary school girl watching "A Baby Story", or a newly divorced woman watching "Say Yes to the Dress?" Of course not. And why is that? That's because these shows don't pertain to them. Who you will see watch "A Baby Story" is a woman who is expecting or who's planning to start a family.

You'll see a newly engaged woman or someone in the throes of planning her wedding, or who is happily married watching "Say Yes to the Dress." That's because it pertains to them. When I was pregnant I had every "A Baby Story" that came on television set to record on DVR. After I had my sons, I wouldn't care to watch "A Baby Story" even if it was the only thing on TV.

    Using that same mentality, we need to watch and invest in the things that pertain to us. Watch the shows that show you how to save, invest, start a business, or launch an idea. Watch "House Hunters" if you dream of owning a home. Watch "Shark Tank" if you dream of turning an invention into a viable product, or into a million dollars. When I was first embracing my desire to become an entrepreneur, I couldn't get enough of a show called "Million Dollar Idea with Donny Deutsch." I watched this show religiously, even taking notes. To this day, I do this kind of thing with the shows that can make me better. And I never miss an opportunity to read a book related to entrepreneurship.

## Read and Digest

Now, by no means am I comparing any book to the Bible. The Bible is the best book ever written, and in my opinion, that will ever be written. But just like we look to the Bible for direction, for clues, for inspiration, for how-to, for what to do, we can look to other books for the same information as it pertains to entrepreneurship.

If you want to be an entrepreneur, read and learn from other entrepreneurs. If you want to be a restaurateur, read and learn from other people who own restaurants. Some people don't like to read. To each his own. But if you're not willing to read a book, then subscribe to a magazine. Or if you don't want to incur the costs of subscribing to a magazine, then try going to Barnes & Noble and sit down and read there. Magazines such as "Black Enterprise" and "Money", magazines on investing, Entrepreneur Magazine, those are all full of information that can help you get from where you are to where you want to be.

Even if you only want to read a little, my belief is that you can still gain a lot. As for me, I never miss an opportunity to read an entrepreneurial book that can enrich my life. As such, I have a full library of such books. If you would like to start your reading journey and find material that can help you advance yourself, just shoot me an e-mail to **info@ttppublishing.com**, and I will recommend some really great skill and business-building books, magazines, or articles to you.

## Chapter 3: Diligently and *INTIMATELY* Prepare for Success

Now that you've studied successful people and shows, whether you know it or not, you have already begun to prepare for success. So step it up. The next step involves preparation. You must prepare mentally, physically, spiritually, and emotionally for the success you can, or are about to receive, as well as for a new person to enter into your life.

**Mental Preparation**

**SEE. BELIEVE. RECEIVE.**

**Activity 2: Write a 1-2 paragraph summary of what your life is, what it entails.**

Hypothetical Example:

I wake up at 6, usually still tired, get the kids ready for school, usually frustrated that I don't get to spend much time with them, or that they're not listening to me, race to a job I tolerate, and sit around people I don't like all day. I live for lunchtime, and the end of the workday, rush to get back home. While at home, I rush to clean, cook dinner, tend to my children, etcetera. I don't make enough money, work too long hours, never take enough (or any) vacations, etcetera.

**OR**

I wake at 9 a.m., sit at home with the kids all day. I run around changing diapers, making bottles, cleaning my home, cooking dinner. I feel like my life is wasting away and that I will never be anything more than a glorified housekeeper. When my significant other gets home from work, I throw the kids off on him/her because I am exhausted. I am depressed. I wish I made my own money, or made more money to contribute to the household. I wish I was living a life that I was proud of. I wish I had an identity.

**OR**

I am in high school/college/graduate school, and although it might sound lazy, I hate waking up early in the morning and going to school, or working for someone, or being in school always preparing to be/do something; I want to be/do something now.

**OR**

I'm tired of struggling …

**OR**

I know/feel like there's something more out there for me. I feel like I am destined for greatness, or I want to live my life to the fullest.

**Activity 3: Now, write down the life you wish you had.**

Hypothetical Example:

I wish I was able to wake when I wanted and spend more time with my kids. I wish I was my own boss and was able to shop at the drop of a dime. I wish I had a nice house that …

## Activity 4: Now, attach pictures to the vision you create for yourself.

Do you want to live on the beach? Go online and look up houses on the beach, or search Yahoo Real Estate and cut out pictures of the houses you see that you like/want. Do you want to travel? Cut out landmarks of the places you want to go. Do you want a life of leisure? Cut out the activities you want to do. Do you want help around the house? Nice cars? Designer clothes? Cut out a maid or butler, the car you want, the clothes/labels you desire.

A great way to keep all this in one place is to either affix all the images to a bulletin board, paste them onto a poster board, or cut them out and put them into plastic sheet protectors and put them into a binder. I use what I call a **"See.Believe.Receive."** binder. I will talk about this in more detail later.

The point of this exercise is to capitalize on the power of faith, visualization, and the power of the tongue. The biblical definition of faith states that

"Now faith is the substance of things hoped for, the evidence of things not seen" (Hebrews 11:1). You may not see any evidence that you will ever be able to purchase your home *outright*, but you start to believe that it will happen. You start to imagine where the mortgage money that had been reserved for the mortgage payment will be reallocated to.

For some of us, not being able to see is a drawback. For those, the **"See.Believe.Receive."** binder works wonders because it allows you to "see" and visualize what will be once you step out on faith and get to work fulfilling your destiny. But remember that "Faith without works is dead" (James 2:20). So you must take an active role in achieving your dreams and fulfilling your destiny. The **"See.Believe.Receive."** binder can help you with that as well.

By stating what you want, and visualizing it, you can then enact your faith that you will get it. I did this before the purchase of my first home. I was young and single, with no help from anyone, and attempting to purchase a 3,000 sq. ft. home all by myself. I would say daily, "I will be a homeowner. I will be a homeowner." I watched House Hunters religiously, and got preapproved while on my lunch break from work. I made a binder with the color schemes that I wanted to put in the house. And when I picked out the home, even before my offer was accepted, I hung out in Home Depot visualizing the remodels I was going to do, because the home was a fixer-upper. Needless to say, at the age of 24, I purchased my first home and have never looked back.

The point is, this strategy works. So let it work for you as you concentrate your efforts on getting prepared to become all that you want to be, and meet the person of your dreams in the process. I do not believe you can go looking for love. Let me rephrase that. I do not believe you will find love if you are out there looking for it. I think what you can do is get yourself ready so that when it finds you, you are a whole person capable of receiving it.

Remember: SEE what you want. BELIEVE you will get it. WORK TO MAKE IT HAPPEN. RECEIVE it.

## Physical Preparation

Now that you're getting the mental preparation together, it's time to focus on the physical. Physical preparation will vary depending on what your goals are. Some physical preparation is general and will vary across goals. For example, it's a good idea to try and get into shape. No, I'm not saying everyone should be a size 2. I am saying that getting in shape gives you energy, releases endorphins, and gets you into the right state of mind. Plus, if you get famous from whatever it is you're doing, you're going to want to look good as you're being interviewed by Barbara Walters or Oprah Winfrey (who is going to come out of retirement just to sit and chat with you). You're going to want to look good as TMZ is following you down the streets of Los Angeles or New York. You don't have to schedule a marathon. Take a walk. Jump rope. Take the stairs instead of the elevator. Do some arm curls with a can of beans as you prepare dinner. Start today.

Some more specific ways in which you can start to physically prepare for your success are related to your goals. If you want to start a baking business, make sure you have a good oven. Make sure you have baking materials. Don't have on press-on nails. Nobody wants to eat your hot pink thumbnail. So make sure it doesn't slip into the batter. Get yourself a cute apron. I firmly believe that dressing the part is half the battle.

If you want to be a hairdresser, make sure your own hair is done. Do not pass out cards in the mall if your hair looks like you just got off a roller coaster. Have a lining if you're going to be a barber. Have a location. Do not bring people to your house to cut their hair or do their hair if your home is not clean. I don't care how well somebody can whip my "do"; if it means I have to sit in a roach-infested house, it means I won't be getting my hair done from them. You don't have to get a shop per se, but arrange a location that speaks to the quality of the service that you provide. It might be a friend's basement, it might be a space you co-share with another professional. The point is to prepare the outside for what is about to come. We all know the importance of first impressions. And whether or not we want to admit it, we have all been guilty of judging a book by its cover. We are visual people. So make that simple fact work for you.

If you are a professional consultant, dress the part, even if it means going to the thrift store to find a cute suit. Do not show up at a professional gig in jeans and cute top. You are not at the movies. Do not show up in six-inch heels that you can't walk in. You are not at the club. If you have gold teeth, please remove them. There is nothing cute about gold, platinum, copper, or psychedelic teeth. Would you go to a dentist with rotten teeth? Would you go to a hairdresser who desperately needs a perm, or a haircut? Or would you let someone work on your natural tresses if their own natural "do" looked dry and brittle? Would you go see a doctor who has a tattoo on his neck?

Look, I am no prude. My belly button has been pierced a long time, and it is still pierced to this day. But you will not know that unless I share that with you. Or unless you see me in a bikini at the beach. You will not see that as I stand in front of you and deliver a talk on the benefits of entrepreneurship. My committee did not see my belly button ring as I stood in front of them and defended my dissertation. My point is, you can express yourself creatively, but always do it while thinking about your end goal. If what you want to do to yourself creatively does not benefit you professionally, then don't do it. In sum, get it together and dress the part.

## Spiritual Preparation

Perhaps the most important way that a person can get themselves together is spiritually. Whether or not you are a Christian, we should all live for a purpose that is greater than ourselves. The purpose you live for might be to make your children proud or to improve their lives; or it might be to give God glory through your life. Whichever the case, realize that purpose and walk into your destiny.

Because I am a Christian, my spiritual preparation might involve seeking God's wisdom and counsel on things I want to do and places I want to go. I know that if I don't check in with Him first, then I will not be as successful. If I don't seek Him first, and instead move on my own accord, then I might lose His favor. And even if (more like when) I achieve worldly success, if I don't have His mercy and grace, then that success might do me more harm than good.

Ultimately, I know that everything I do should be to give Him glory. So my spiritual preparation, in essence, is a map letting me know when I do - or making sure I don't - go off course. If what I am doing will not give Him glory, then I know that I am not doing the right thing. But if your faith is different, spiritual preparation is still necessary. If your spirit-man seeks peace, then you have to make sure that what you do lines up with that. I could be wrong, but if your spirit-man seeks peace, it's probably not a good idea to run a Fortune 500 company. Or to be responsible for an organization that employs hundreds of people. With such a career you would probably be responsible for making really big decisions. The kind of decisions that have life changing consequences and that affect a lot of people. I don't know that such a career would bring peace. But like I said, I could be wrong.

The basic point is to make sure that your whole self is in agreement as you move forward in your endeavor. Your mental, physical, and spiritual parts need to be on the same page if you are to achieve, and indeed enjoy, success.

## Emotional Preparation

We all have a little crazy in us. If you want to see my mild crazy, then come into my home and make a mess. Or do something gross in my presence. But if you want to see my for real, full-blast crazy, then bother one of my children. Or my family. Mama bears ain't got nothing on me.

Sometimes, as is the case with protecting our children for example, crazy if necessary. Other times, it's meaningless and a waste of productive energy. Take my need to keep my home clean. I have a husband and two sons. Does that say enough? For those of you who didn't get the significance of that statement, to put it plainly, there are some days I spend the whole day just in the pursuit of a clean home. Had I refocused my energy, who's to say I couldn't have finished a few pages of a book, or thought up a wonderful new program to add to my Institute, or better yet, just sat down and enjoyed my messy home with my beautiful family?

Emotionally, at least for me, a clean home represents a clean mind. It represents organization and structure, and to an extent, control. With a clean home I can focus on other things. My obsession with cleanliness is such that I will sometimes get upset with my husband because he's left too many things out around the house, or frustrated with my four-year-old after I've stepped on one of his cars for the fourth time. My OCD-ish need for a clean home is emotional junk. And sometimes our emotional junk costs a high price. It might cost productivity, it might cost us our peace. Truth be told, it won't kill me if my home is out of order. Or, if after a morning of fishing in the lake behind our home, my husband tracks mud across the floor. Or if my four-year-old gets crayons on the wall. Or if my 4 month old spits up on the sofa. Sometimes it's best to clear our mind of impossible expectations, and let ourselves – and those around us - off the hook a little.

For you this might look like forgiving yourself for not finishing college, yet still deciding that even without a college degree you're going to be successful. Or it might be forgiving a person who has hurt you. I don't advise letting them hurt you again. But forgive them, because that forgiveness is not for them. Forgive them so that you can have the mental space necessary to move on and achieve your goals.

    A great way to clean out your emotional closet is to talk to someone professionally. Having been in that field myself for a number of years, I know that it can be expensive. If finances are a concern, then look to your church for help working through your emotional issues. If you don't belong to a church, then journal. Writing down what you feel, how you feel, and why, is wonderfully therapeutic. Write down what you feel, look for themes, analyze and speculate on the origin of those issues, problem solve, pray, move on.

    Although this is a very simplified way of stating it, the point is, address your emotional issues in any way that you can so that you can clean out some of your baggage and make room for new opportunities and new growth.

## Chapter 4: *COMMIT* to your goals and get what you want

This final chapter involves combining all the previously discussed steps and producing a well-oiled machine: You. The steps involve:

1. **Finding out what you love to do and doing it well, monetizing it, and becoming your own CEO**
2. **Getting rid of people, places, and things that hold you back**
3. **Beginning to prepare mentally, physically, spiritually, and emotionally for your success**
4. **Committing and recommitting every day to doing something towards achieving, maintaining, and/or growing your goals and dreams. Become allergic to mediocrity!**
5. **And then, when you least expect it because you've been so busy doing your own thing and getting your life together,** *here he or*

***she comes*, so step 5 is to email me with your success story☺.**

In conclusion: Good luck, God bless, get yours and you'll likely get him (or her) too.

## About TTP Publishing

*"Providing short and sweet books you can enjoy, when you're ready to enjoy them, that WON'T take all day...*

**...BECAUSE YOU HAVE THINGS TO DO"**

TTP Publishing is a book and media publishing company that specializes in publishing short books. It was founded by an avid reader who, after becoming a mom, doctor, bill-payer, and errand-runner, realized she had little to no time left in a day to sit back and enjoy a good book.

What's more, this busy mom was also impatient, meaning she not only wanted to sit back and enjoy a good book with her limited "me" time, but she also wanted to reach the conclusion of that book - without having to wait days or even weeks before she had more time to read again.

This busy mom had an "aha" moment as she thought of how awesome it would be if good books were shorter and lasted the length of say, a good movie, or dinner out.

That's when **TTP Publishing** - "TTP" stands for **to the point** - was founded.

TTP's books are sometimes funny, sometimes controversial, sometimes spicy, and sometimes tell-it-like-it-is, but they are almost always short and to the point...*because you have things to do.*

For information on submitting your book for publication, please visit us at www.ttppublishing.com, or send us an email to info@ttppublishing.com.

Happy Reading!!!

## TTP Publishing Books

*Act Like a CEO, Think Like a Millionaire: Why You Should Care LESS About What a Man or Woman Thinks About Love, Relationships, Intimacy and Commitment and MORE About GETTING WHAT YOU WANT OUT OF LIFE*

*What You WON'T Expect When You're Expecting Because This is The CRAP They Don't Tell You: ABC's of a Sucky Pregnancy*

*Confessions of a Surrogate for Celebrities*

*TESTIMONY: 10 Stories Detailing Supernatural Miracles, Blessings, and THE POWER OF PRAYER*

*Open Marriage: An Erotic Trilogy* (Book 1)

*Open Marriage: A.S.E. Sports Agency* (Book 2)

*Open Marriage: Behind the Scenes* (Book 3)

www.ingramcontent.com/pod-product-compliance
Lightning Source LLC
Chambersburg PA
CBHW071313060426
42444CB00034B/2128